CAMBRIDGE
UNIVERSITY PRESS

Coding Club

Python: Next Steps

level

Chris Roffey

CAMBRIDGE UNIVERSITY PRESS
Cambridge, New York, Melbourne, Madrid, Cape Town,
Singapore, São Paulo, Delhi, Mexico City

Cambridge University Press
The Edinburgh Building, Cambridge CB2 8RU, UK

www.cambridge.org
Information on this title: www.cambridge.org/9781107623255

First published 2013

Printed in Poland by Opolgraf

A catalogue record for this publication is available from the British Library

ISBN 978-1-107-62325-5 Paperback

Contents

Introduction

Who is this book for?

This book is the Level 2 core book in the *Coding Club* series of books. To get the most out of this title, you should be familiar with the Python 3 programming language and know about variables, while loops and if, elif and else statements. Therefore, we advise that you first read *Python Basics* before reading this book. *Python: Next steps* is aimed at 12–13 year olds but is accessible to older children and even adults who want to learn about computer programming.

Why should you choose this book?

This book explains important principles while helping you build useful short projects. We want you, the reader, to learn not only how to make the programs in this book but also how to design your own. We want you to be able to write programs well, so that if you take it further and become the inventor of the next Google you will not have to unlearn bad programming habits.

What you need?

Any computer can run Python 3. If your computer does not already have Python 3 installed there is a section on the companion website (www.codingclub.co.uk) that guides you through the installation. This takes about five minutes! That is all you need to get started.

Start files for all the projects in the book are available to download from the companion website so you do not get lost in the bigger projects. There are also finished files for each project, should you get stuck, and answers to the puzzles and challenges.

How to use this book

You should read this book carefully and build all the main projects in order. At the end of each chapter there are further ideas, and challenges that you can think of as 'mini quests'. Some readers will want to work through them all so that they understand everything all the time. Some of you will probably prefer to rush through and get to the end. Which approach is best? The one you are most comfortable with is the best approach for you. If you are being guided by a teacher, you should trust their judgement so that you can get the most help out of them as possible.

There are four ways in which this book tries to help you to learn:

1 Typing in the code – this is important as it gets you to work through the code a line at a time (like computers do) and will help you remember the details in the future.
2 Finding and fixing errors – error messages in Python give you some clues as to what has gone wrong. Solving these problems yourself will help you to be a better programmer. However, if you get stuck, the code can be downloaded from the companion website (www.codingclub.co.uk).

3 Experimenting – feel free to experiment with the code you write. See what else you can make it do. If you try all the challenges, puzzles and ideas, and generally play with the code, this will help you learn how to write code like a professional.

4 Finally, this book will not only provide the code to build some pretty cool, short projects – it will also teach you how the programs were designed. You can then use the same methods to design your own applications.

A word of warning

You may be tempted to simply get the code off the website instead of typing it out yourself. If you do this you will probably find that you cannot remember how to write code so easily later. In this book you will only be asked to type small chunks of code at a time – remember that this will help you understand every detail of each of your programs.

Chapter 1
Data types

In this chapter you will:

- learn about data types

- learn about tuples, lists and dictionaries

- make a version of MyMagic8Ball that is much shorter than the one from *Python Basics*.

Data types

In *Python Basics* you learned about **strings** (bits of text), **integers** (whole numbers) and **floats** (numbers with a decimal point). These are examples of **data types**. There are more! In this chapter we will look at some new data types: tuples, lists and dictionaries. These new data types are all called **container** data types because they store more than one piece of data. For example, they can store several strings. They do so in different ways and have their own advantages and disadvantages.

A string is rather like a container because it stores a whole sequence of letters or numbers (or a mixture of both). In *Python Basics* we learned that there are several functions we can use on strings. We can also use many of these functions on tuples, lists and dictionaries.

I'm back!

Tuples

A **tuple** is the simplest of our new data types. They can store strings, integers and other data types. Here is an example of a tuple that stores four strings, each separated by a comma:

```
my_tuple = ("one", "two", "three", "four")
```

Each **value** in a tuple is separated by a comma. Unlike variables, we cannot change what is stored in a given tuple.

Each value in the tuple has an **index** starting from 0. So, print(my_tuple[1]) for the example above produces the **output** two. Look at how this works below.

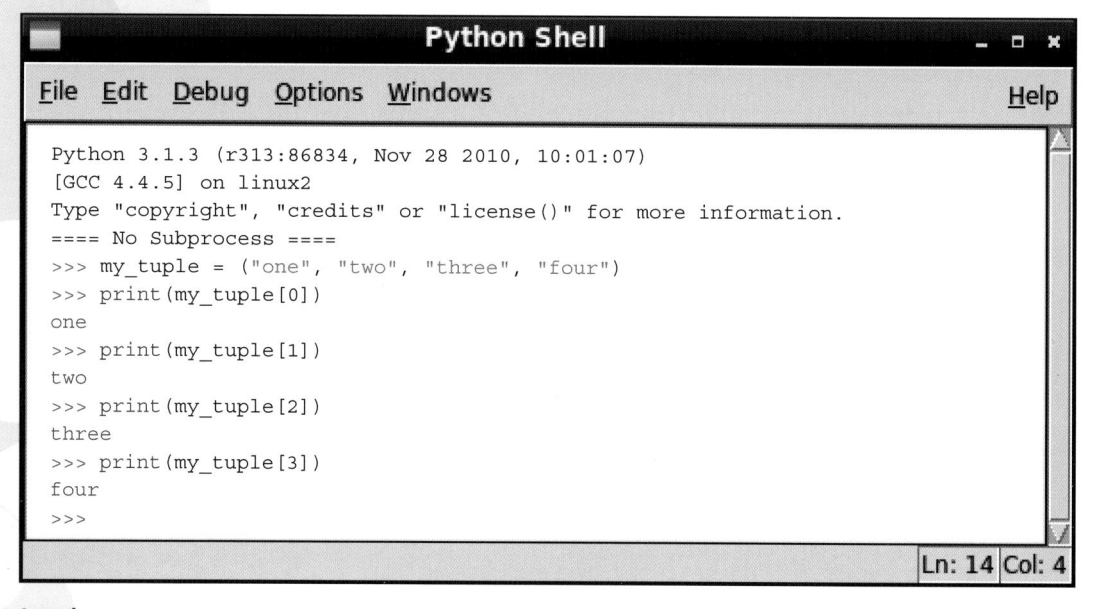

```
Python 3.1.3 (r313:86834, Nov 28 2010, 10:01:07)
[GCC 4.4.5] on linux2
Type "copyright", "credits" or "license()" for more information.
==== No Subprocess ====
>>> my_tuple = ("one", "two", "three", "four")
>>> print(my_tuple[0])
one
>>> print(my_tuple[1])
two
>>> print(my_tuple[2])
three
>>> print(my_tuple[3])
four
>>>
```

A tuple.

MyMagic8Ball

In *Python Basics* we wrote a small application called MyMagic8Ball that used the random **module** and the functions `print()`, `input()` and `randint()`. Here is the code:

Code Box 1.1

```python
# My Magic 8 Ball

import random

# write answers
ans1="Go for it!"
ans2="No way, Jose!"
ans3="I'm not sure. Ask me again."
ans4="Fear of the unknown is what imprisons us."
ans5="It would be madness to do that!"
ans6="Only you can save mankind!"
ans7="Makes no difference to me, do or don't - whatever."
ans8="Yes, I think on balance that is the right choice."

print("Welcome to MyMagic8Ball.")

# get the user's question
question = input("Ask me for advice then press ENTER to shake me.\n")
```

(continues on the next page)

```python
print("shaking ...\n" * 4)

# use the randint() function to select the correct answer
choice=random.randint(1, 8)
if choice==1:
    answer=ans1
elif choice==2:
    answer=ans2
elif choice==3:
    answer=ans3
elif choice==4:
    answer=ans4
elif choice==5:
    answer=ans5
elif choice==6:
    answer=ans6
elif choice==7:
    answer=ans7
else:
    answer=ans8

# print the answer to the screen
print(answer)

input("\n\nPress the RETURN key to finish.")
```

Now see how much easier and shorter the code is if we include a tuple:

```python
# My Magic 8 Ball

import random

# put answers in a tuple

answers = (
    "Go for it!",
    "No way, Jose!",
    "I'm not sure. Ask me again.",
    "Fear of the unknown is what imprisons us.",
    "It would be madness to do that!",
    "Only you can save mankind!",
    "Makes no difference to me, do or don't - whatever.",
    "Yes, I think on balance that is the right choice."
    )

print("Welcome to MyMagic8Ball.")

# get the user's question
question = input("Ask me for advice then press ENTER to shake me.\n")

print("shaking ...\n" * 4)

# use the randint() function to select the correct answer
choice = random.randint(0, 7)
```

(continues on the next page)

```
# print the answer to the screen
print(answers[choice])

# exit nicely
input("\n\nPress the RETURN key to finish.")
```

Analysis of Code Box 1.2

If it has been a while since you read *Python Basics*, you might find it useful to type this code into IDLE and think about it line by line. Here is what it does.

The import statement

We are going to use a **function** from Python's random module so we need to import it.

The tuple

We have to separate the strings in the tuple `answers` with commas. Starting a new line after each comma makes the code much easier to read.

The input() function

The `input()` function listens to the keyboard entry and waits for the **return** key to be pressed. It then returns the keyboard input as a string, which we store in the **variable** `question`.

```
question = input("Ask me for advice then press ENTER to shake me.\n")
```

variable name to access
the keyboard input

string that is printed out,
giving instructions to the user

The randint() function

```
choice = random.randint(0, 7)
```

This line of code asks the randint() **method** in the random module to select a random number from 0 to 7. This number is then stored in the variable called choice. (A method is a function in a class.)

Finishing off

```
print(answers[choice])
```

This uses the random number choice as the index in the answers tuple. This line selects the string that was randomly chosen from the tuple and prints it.

Experiment

The two scripts are available from the companion website (www.codingclub.co.uk). Try them both out and check that they do the same thing.

Are you are a bit confused about when to use round brackets and when to use square brackets? Basically, when we create a tuple we wrap its contents in round brackets. Whenever we call an indexed value from the tuple, we put the index (its position in the list) in square brackets.

Lists

A **list** is another type of container. They are very similar to tuples except that they can be altered. Think of tuples as quick, memory-efficient lists that cannot be altered by other code. We cannot insert or delete items in tuples with our programs. There are, however, functions to allow us to insert or delete items in lists. Lists are written like this:

```
my_list = ["one", "two", "three", "four"]
```

Just as with tuples, each value in the list has an index starting from 0 and each value is separated by a comma.

Look at how this works in **interactive mode**:

```
>>> my_list = ["one", "two", "three", "four"]
>>> my_list[2]
'three'
>>> my_tuple = ("one", "two", "three", "four")
>>> my_tuple[2]
'three'
>>>
```

You can see that both a list and a tuple provide the same output. So, when would we use a list instead of a tuple? We would choose a list rather than a tuple if we want our program to add, remove or change an item within the list.

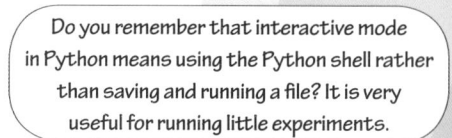

Hmm, the list is surrounded by square brackets this time.

Do you remember that interactive mode in Python means using the Python shell rather than saving and running a file? It is very useful for running little experiments.

For each of the following say which is the best choice, a list or a tuple:

1 A place to store seven strings consisting of the days of the week (e.g. `"Monday"`) that we want to use in an application.
2 A place to store the full names of members of the Coding Club in an application we use to keep track of who is still a club member.
3 A place to store the ten integer values (0, 1, 2, 3, 4, 5, 6, 7, 8 and 9) of the keys used to make a calculator app.

Dictionaries

The last of our container data types is a **dictionary**. Dictionaries take a slightly different form. In dictionaries we supply our own indexes. Here, we call the index a **key**. Keys can be strings, integers, floats or even tuples. Here is an example:

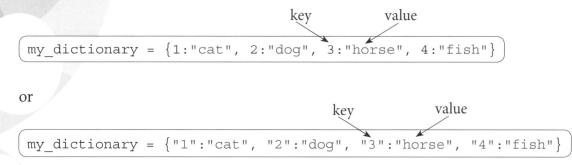

```
my_dictionary = {1:"cat", 2:"dog", 3:"horse", 4:"fish"}
```

or

```
my_dictionary = {"1":"cat", "2":"dog", "3":"horse", "4":"fish"}
```

Silly me, I was confused for a moment here as I had forgotten that strings always appear in speech marks and numbers do not. So 1 is an integer but "1" is a number stored as a string!

Look at how this works in interactive mode:

```
>>> my_dictionary = {1:"one", 2:"two", 3:"three", 4:"four"}
>>> my_dictionary[2]
'two'
>>> my_dictionary = {"1":"one", "2":"two", "3":"three", "4":"four"}
>>> my_dictionary["2"]
'two'
```

You might have noticed that dictionaries require a different structure within the brackets to assign keys to the values. They use a colon ':' to separate the value from its key.

What's with the brackets?

When we create a new container, Python provides us with a quick way of defining which kind we require by our choice of brackets.

- If you want a tuple – wrap it in round brackets.

- If you want a list – use square brackets.

- If it's a dictionary you are after – use curly brackets.

What's the difference?

Strings, tuples and lists are all indexed **ordered containers**; the values are automatically given an index based on the order in which they were input. Dictionaries have keys that *you* provide and the key–value pairs are *not* stored in a particular order. Strings and tuples have their content set at creation and cannot be changed by a program directly. Lists and dictionaries are containers in which the values can be added to and changed in a variety of ways.

It is also possible to create empty containers like this:

```
my_string = ""
my_tuple = ()
my_list = []
my_dictionary = {}
```

Useful functions

Table 1.1 provides a list of useful functions you can use on strings, tuples, lists and dictionaries. You can also find it in Appendix 1. The table assumes the following containers have been created:

```
>>> s = "bar" # a string
>>> t = ("b", "a", "r") # a tuple
>>> l = ["b", "a", "r"] # a list
>>> d = {1:"b", 2:"a", 3:"r"} # a dictionary
```

Function	Strings	Tuples	Lists	Dictionaries
print all	`>>> print(s)` `bar`	`>>> print(t)` `('b', 'a', 'r')`	`>>> print(l)` `['b', 'a', 'r']`	`>>> print(d)` `{1: 'b', 2: 'a', 3: 'r'}`
print element	`>>> print(s[2])` `r`	`>>> print(t[2])` `r`	`>>> print(l[2])` `r`	`>>> print(d[2])` `a`

combine	`>>> a=s+"f"`
	`>>> a`
	`'barf'`
		`>>> a=t+("f",)`
		`>>> a`
		`('b', 'a', 'r', 'f')`
			`>>> a=l+["f"]`
			`>>> a`
			`['b', 'a', 'r', 'f']`	

add an element	Strings cannot be altered.	Tuples cannot be altered.	`>>> l.append("f")`
			`>>> l`
			`['b', 'a', 'r', 'f']`
				`>>> d[4]="f"`
				`>>> d[4]`
				`'f'`

sort	Strings cannot be altered.	Tuples cannot be altered.	`>>> l.sort()`
			`>>> l`
			`['a', 'b', 'r']`
				`>>> sorted(d)`
				`['1', '2', '3']`
				`>>> sorted(d.values())`
				`['a', 'b', 'r']`

delete an element	Strings cannot be altered.	Tuples cannot be altered.	`>>> del l[1]`
			`>>> l`
			`['b', 'r']`
				`>>> del d[1]`
				`>>> i`
				`{2:'a', 3:'r'}`

replace element	Strings cannot be altered.	Tuples cannot be altered.	`>>> l[0]="c"`
			`>>> l`
			`['c', 'a', 'r']`
				`>>> d[1]="c"`
				`>>> print(d)`
				`{1: 'c', 2: 'a', 3: 'r'}`

find	`>>> i.find("b")` `0`	`>>> t.index("b")` `0`	`>>> l.index("b")` `0`	
get length	`>>> len(s)` `3`	`>>> len(t)` `3`	`>>> len(l)` `3`	`>>> len(d)` `3`

Table 1.1 Some useful functions.

> This table could be very helpful when I write my own applications!

```
s = "bar" # a string
t = ("b", "a", "r") # a tuple
l = ["b", "a", "r"] # a list
d = {1:"b", 2:"a", 3:"r"} # a dictionary
```

For each of the following say whether to choose a tuple, a list, or a dictionary:

1 A container to store the personal best times achieved by club swimmers in the 100m freestyle such as: Mark: 65.34s, Freya: 68.04s, etc.
2 A container to store the months of the year.
3 A container to store the monthly rainfall data for London in 2012.
4 A container to store the names of the students who currently attend the chess club.

Chapter summary

In this chapter you have:

- learned more about data types
- learned about tuples, lists and dictionaries
- made a shorter version of MyMagic8Ball
- seen some of the different functions that can and cannot be used with the new data types.

We will explore these new data types further in this book. Here are just a few ideas that will help you refresh your coding skills from *Python Basics*. (As dictionaries are the hardest to use, we will wait until you have learned a little bit more before providing any puzzles involving them.)

It is always good to practise.

Puzzle

Write a new version of MyMagic8Ball using a list instead of a tuple. It should work in exactly the same way if you get it right because lists can do everything tuples can and more.

Challenge

This is a challenge from *Python Basics* so although you may be a bit rusty you should be able to manage it. Hopefully it brings back happy memories for you.

1 Add some code to `myMagic8Ball2.py` (Code Box 1.2) so that the Magic8Ball says "Hi" and asks for the user's name at the start of the game.
2 It should then store the input in a variable such as `user_name`.
3 Change the code so that the Magic8Ball talks to the user using their name. At the end for example, it could say: "Thanks for playing, [Name]. Please press the RETURN key to finish."

There are several ways to do this.

To see one answer go to www.codingclub.co.uk/book2_resources.php.

You are destined to become a famous computer scientist one day!

Idea

Change the Magic8Ball game into a fortune cookie game. You could call it `myFortuneCookie.py`.

Chapter 2
Building GUIs

In this chapter you will:

- practise using tuples and dictionaries

- revise how to use tkinter and learn about using widgets

- build a graphical user interface (GUI)

- build a glossary application.

MyGlossary

A graphical user interface (**GUI**) is, very simply, the 'screen' that allows a user to interact with their computer through graphics such as menus and buttons. You are now going to build a small GUI application of your own using **tkinter**.

In the source code downloaded from the companion website, in the folder for Chapter 2, you will find a file called myGlossary_Start.py. This file provides you with outline source code for a glossary application containing the complete glossary for this book. This is also provided for reference in Code Box 2.1.

Code Box 2.1

```
# myGlossary_Start.py

from tkinter import *

# key press function:

##### main:
window = Tk()
window.title("My Coding Club Glossary")

# create label

# create text entry box

# Add a submit button:
```

```
# create another label

# create text box

# The dictionary:
my_glossary = {
    'algorithm': 'Step by step instructions to perform a task that a
computer could understand.',
    'bug': 'A piece of code that is causing a program to fail to run
properly or at all.',
    'binary number': 'A number represented in base 2.'
    }

##### Run mainloop
window.mainloop()
```

It is useful to be able to choose whether to wrap strings in single or double speech marks. Don't forget to be consistent in your code though.

The glossary has been stored as a dictionary data type. The key is the glossary word and the **value** is the definition.

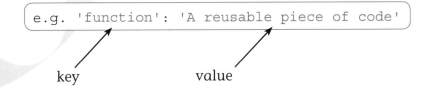

```
e.g. 'function': 'A reusable piece of code'
```

key   value

We have used single speech marks rather than the usual double ones so that we can use double speech marks in the definitions without having to **escape** them all.

To access the definition for a glossary term, all that is required is to write code that is something like this:

```
print(my_glossary["function"])
```

If you run `myGlossary_Start.py` as it is supplied, it should open a small window entitled 'My Coding Club Glossary'.

tkinter widgets

In *Python Basics* you were introduced to tkinter and you learned how to use this module to open a window. We then used tkinter's Canvas class to provide an area where we could draw. Canvas is an example of a tkinter **widget**. tkinter provides all the normal widgets that are available in modern programming languages, such as buttons, labels or text entry fields. Indeed there are popular alternatives to tkinter even in Python.

> I often use widgets in my web apps. The main widgets I use are buttons, checkboxes, bullet lists, dropdown menus and textboxes.

Delving Deeper

Although all modern languages provide these GUI facilities they do not all do so in the same way as tkinter. If in the future you want to create an application in a different programming language, you will need to find out how it provides windows, canvases, buttons, labels, etc. To do this, read the documentation for the GUI library you choose to use.

In this section you will learn about some more tkinter widgets and see how to build a simple GUI. First we must see how tkinter arranges things in the window we have created. The window is divided into as many columns and rows as we require. Each row and column is numbered so that the cells can be referenced by coordinates in the usual computer science way – (0,0) from the top left:

(0,0)	(0,1)	(0,2)
(1,0)	(1,1)	(1,2)
(2,0)	(2,1)	(2,2)

A tkinter grid.

In addition to assigning a cell for our widgets, we can determine where we put them inside these cells by making them stick to the north (top), south (bottom), west (left) or east (right) of the cells. It is easier to see this in action.

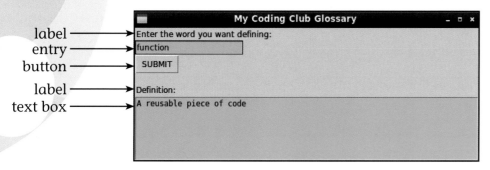

tkinter widgets.

The Label widget

The Label widget is probably the simplest one. It just provides some text in the application window. In `myGlossary_Start.py`, add the code from Code Box 2.2 under the `# create label` comment.

```
Code Box 2.2                                                                    x

 Label(window, text="Enter the word you want defining:").grid(row=0, column=0, sticky=W)
```

`W` stands for west. If you save and run this now you will see how it works.

The Entry widget

The Entry widget provides a box for entering text. It could be added in exactly the same way as the label widget. However, as your code is going to have to refer to this box later, it is best to assign the widget a name with the **equals operator**. We will call this text entry box, `entry`.

In `myGlossary_Start.py` add the code from Code Box 2.3 under the `# create text entry box` comment.

```
Code Box 2.3                                                          x

 entry = Entry(window, width=20, bg="light green")
 entry.grid(row=1, column=0, sticky=W)
```

Delving Deeper

Compare the last two code boxes carefully to see the two different ways of using the dot operator. Again, if you save and run the code, you will see how it works. In Code Box 2.1 we did not give the label a variable name because we are not going to want to call on it later. Hence, we use the dot operator to call the `grid()` method, which will assign the tkinter position values. All of tkinter's widget classes have a `grid()` method we can use. In Code Box 2.2, we create the text entry box and assign it to a variable name so that we can call on it elsewhere in our code. The code is then neater and easier to read if we use the dot operator to assign the position variables on the next line attaching them to the text box name, `entry`.

Experiment

Try rewriting the code you have added in Code Box 2.3 in the same way as in Code Box 2.2 like this:

Code Box 2.4

```
entry = Entry(window, width=20, bg="light green").grid(row=1,
              column=0, sticky=W)
```

(continues on the next page)

Does it make any difference?

Important: You will find at this stage that it does not seem to make any difference but in fact it does! If you leave the code like this and do not put it back to how it was, you will find it comes back and bites you later with a **bug** that is very difficult to spot. What happens is, if we add the `grid()` method at the end of the line with the dot operator, it succeeds in creating the text box but fails to assign it to the variable called `entry`. So when we finish our `click()` method we will keep being told that `entry` does not exist. In other words, please make sure the code is back like it was in Code Box 2.3 before moving on.

The Button widget

The Button widget provides a button! We want it to do something when we press it, so before we make the button let's just add the beginning of the function it will call when it is pressed. Add the code from Code Box 2.5 just below the `# key press function` comment.

Code Box 2.5

```
# key press function
def click():
    entered_text = entry.get() # collect text from text entry box
```

Now just below the `# Add a submit button` comment, add the code from Code Box 2.6.

Code Box 2.6

```
# Add a submit button
Button(window, text="SUBMIT", width=5, command=click).grid(row=2, column=0, sticky=W)
```

As with all the other widgets, the first **argument** (information required by a function or widget) is `window`, which tells tkinter where the widget is to be placed. `command=click` tells the button to call the `click()` function when the button is pressed. Notice how you must not include the brackets when assigning the function to the button. If you do include them it tries to run the function when the button is created rather than when it is pressed. We will use buttons a lot in later chapters where we will be able to see how this works more clearly. Finally, we call the Button class's `grid()` method to place it where we want it in the window. You can run this to see a pretty useless button if you want to check everything so far.

The Text widget

Add another label and then a text box by entering the code from Code Box 2.7 in the appropriate sections in `myGlossary_Start.py`. You should understand this code by now.

Code Box 2.7

```
# create another label
Label(window, text="\nDefinition:").grid(row=3, column=0, sticky=W)

# create text box
output = Text(window, width=75, height=6, wrap=WORD, background="light green")
output.grid(row=4, column=0, columnspan=2, sticky=W)
```

Again it is possible to run this code but do not expect a great deal to happen, as our `click()` function is not finished. The application does however have all of its widgets and so the GUI is complete.

It does not do much but it is beginning to look good.

Finishing off MyGlossary

The only thing left to do is to complete the `click()` function. This will call the definition we want from our dictionary. Complete the `click()` function by entering the code from Code Box 2.8.

Code Box 2.8

```python
# key press function
def click():
    entered_text = entry.get() # collect text from text entry box
    output.delete(0.0, END) # clear text box
    definition = my_glossary[entered_text]
    output.insert(END, definition)
```

Analysis of Code Box 2.8

`entry.get()` applies the `get()` function to the `entry` widget. This collects whatever text has been typed in to this text entry box and assigns it to the `entered_text` variable.

Next we clear the text box widget called `output` with this widget's `delete()` method. This takes two arguments. The `0.0` says start deleting from line 0 (i.e. before line 1) and before character 0 (i.e. the beginning). `END` is a **constant** that always refers to the position after the last character in the text box. We could also have replaced `END` with a `line.character` index but `END` is easier.

Delving Deeper

The indexes referred to in the `delete()` method work like coordinates but actually indicate where the cursor goes when selecting text. The rows or lines count from 0, before the first line, then 1 is the first line, 2 is the next etc. The character index (or column index) counts from 0, before the first character, then 1 after it, 2 next etc. Don't forget a space is a character.

For example, `my_string = "text|widget box"` the cursor is at index position (1.4).

The next line of code finds the definition in the dictionary using the entered text as the key. Finally, this is added to the text box widget called `output` using the widget's `insert()` method. This takes two arguments:

1 where to start the insertion: `(END)` i.e. the beginning (we have just cleared `output`)
2 what to insert: the definition found in the dictionary in the previous line.

Did you know that the glossary contains all the key words from this book and *Python Basics*?

Testing

Try this out by saving and running the program. Once it is running try entering the word 'bug' and pressing the SUBMIT button. If this works delete 'bug' and try 'function'. All good so far? Now let's test it with nothing added and with some random key presses that do not make up a word. These do not cause the app to crash completely but the console starts to spin with errors because the search through the dictionary fails.

Catching errors

It is good practice to think of all the things that can go wrong in your programs and handle them. Python provides us with a way of doing this that is very helpful. It uses `try:` and `except:`. The fix to the `click()` function is provided in Code Box 2.9. Study it carefully and then correct and save the `myGlossary_Start.py` application.

Code Box 2.9

```python
# key press function
def click():
    entered_text = entry.get() # collect text from text entry box
    output.delete(0.0, END) # clear text box
    try:
        definition = my_glossary[entered_text]
    except:
        definition = "There is no entry for this word."
    output.insert(END, definition)
```

This completes the program. You now have a handy little application that you can have available while reading this book. You can use it to look up any **bold** words you find in this book that you are unsure of.

Chapter summary

In this chapter you have:

- practised using dictionaries
- revised how to use tkinter and learned about some more widgets
- built a GUI
- built a glossary application.

Combining dictionaries and GUIs is very powerful and should allow you to make many little applications. Here are some ideas.

Idea 1

Using the glossary program as a template, make some revision flash cards to help you revise.

Flash cards.

Idea 2

Using the glossary program as a template, make a vocabulary app to help you with a foreign language you are studying. Make the key the English word and the definition the translation.

My French Vocab App
GET Question   NEXT
school
GET ANSWER
Answer:
l'école

Vocab app.

Challenge

Using the glossary program as a template, make a quiz app that selects random questions and provides the answers when you press GET ANSWER.
Hint: You will need two text boxes rather than one entry box and one text box. You will also need a NEXT button, in addition to the GET ANSWER one. To see one answer go to www.codingclub.co.uk.

My Quiz App
GET Question   NEXT
What is a function?
GET ANSWER
Answer:
A function is a reusable piece of code.

Quiz app.

Idea 3

Using the solution from the challenge as a template, make a random joke generator.

Hint: You will need to stick to two-liners like this:

Q: What do you get if you cross a coder and a footballer?

A: Foot oder

My Joke App — □ ✕

| GET JOKE | | GET ANSWER |

Why did the scarecrow get a gold medal?

Answer:

He was outstanding in his field.

Joke generator app.

Chapter 3
Designing a simple calculator

In this chapter you will:

- learn about how loops work

- use lists and loops to save a lot of repetitive coding

- learn more about the tkinter button widget

- design your own calculator application called MyCalculator

- build a complex GUI easily.

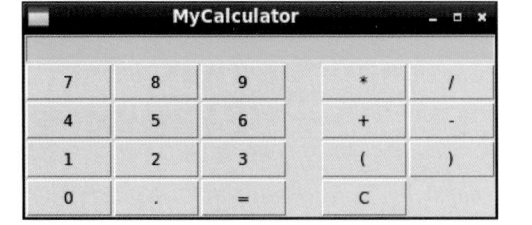

Laying out the calculator

In this chapter we are going to lay out a simple calculator. This is just the beginning! Later in the book we will add some more buttons so that you can customise it. Very soon you will have built a fully programmable calculator.

This chapter focuses on making a neat layout as efficiently as possible. As there are a lot of similar buttons, you will build them by looping though lists rather than one at a time. With this new knowledge you will be able to build all sorts of new applications that users can easily interact with.

Starting the design

Investigation 1

First we will try to build the calculator one button at a time. Do not worry – most of the work has been done for you. Open `myCalculator_expt1.py` from the folder for Chapter 3 supplied on the companion website. You will find the code for a calculator app that has one button and a display (Code Box 3.1).

```
Code Box 3.1

# myCalculator_expt1.py

from tkinter import *
from decimal import *

##### main:
window = Tk()
window.title("MyCalculator")
```

(continues on the next page)

```
# use Entry widget for an editable display
display = Entry(window, width=45, bg="light green")
display.grid()

# create num_pad buttons:
def click1():
    display.insert(END, "1")

Button(window, text="1", width=5, command=click1).grid(row=1,column=0)


##### Run mainloop
window.mainloop()
```

If you press the button, it will output the string `"1"` to the display. Run the application and check that it functions as expected. Look at the code carefully and try adding a second button – the 2 button. Try to do this and add a third button before looking below at the supplied answer.

Now compare your code with the solution in Code Box 3.2:

Code Box 3.2

```
# create num_pad buttons:
def click1():
    display.insert(END, "1")
Button(window, text="1", width=5, command=click1).grid(row=1,column=0)
```

```
def click2():
    display.insert(END, "2")
Button(window, text="2", width=5, command=click2).grid(row=2,column=0)

def click3():
    display.insert(END, "3")
Button(window, text="3", width=5, command=click3).grid(row=3,column=0)
```

Analysis of Code Box 3.2

For each button we are adding three lines of code. There are 19 buttons on the simple calculator and in the next chapter we will add another 10. This will result in a lot of copying and pasting and leads to many lines of code. This method of programming becomes annoying when you wish to change the design. For example, if you wanted to change the width of the buttons, you would have to change the code for width in 29 sets of buttons! Furthermore, most of the buttons do the same thing: they add their value to the display. It makes sense therefore to have one function that handles button clicks and put it at the top of our code listing.

Investigation 2

In this investigation we will try to build the number pad with a **loop**. Open myCalculator_expt2.py from the Chapter 3 folder. You can see the code below in Code Box 3.3. This produces a calculator application that has nine buttons and a display. Can you see how we have used counter variables for the rows and columns and how these are increased to build the number pad? Notice also that when you run it, the buttons do not appear to do anything when you press them.

This is an example of what computer scientists call refactoring – it is an important skill for coders to learn.

Code Box 3.3

```python
# myCalculator_expt2.py

from tkinter import *
from decimal import *

# key press function:
def click(key):
    display.insert(END, key)

##### main:
window = Tk()
window.title("MyCalculator")

# create top_row frame
top_row = Frame(window)
top_row.grid(row=0, column=0, columnspan=2, sticky=N)

# use Entry widget for an editable display
display = Entry(top_row, width=45, bg="light green")
display.grid()

# create num_pad_frame
num_pad = Frame(window)
num_pad.grid(row=1, column=0, sticky=W)
```

```
# provide a list of keys for the number pad:
num_pad_list = [
'7', '8', '9',
'4', '5', '6',
'1', '2', '3',
'0', '.', '=' ]

# create num_pad buttons with a loop
r = 0 # row counter
c = 0 # column counter

for btn_text in num_pad_list:
    Button(num_pad, text=btn_text, width=5, command=click(btn_text)).grid(row=r, column=c)
    c = c+1
    if c > 2:
        c = 0
        r = r+1

##### Run mainloop
window.mainloop()
```

Deliberate mistake!

↓

? Quick Quiz 3.1

What is the deliberate mistake?

(Leave the code as shown – we will look into this more in the testing and debugging section.)

Using frames

While you were trying out Investigation 1, you may have tried putting the three buttons next to each other and found that they did not fit very well. One way of controlling groups of elements is by spanning columns. But it is often better to put groups of widgets in another widget called a **frame**. This is how we will use frames to organise the calculator.

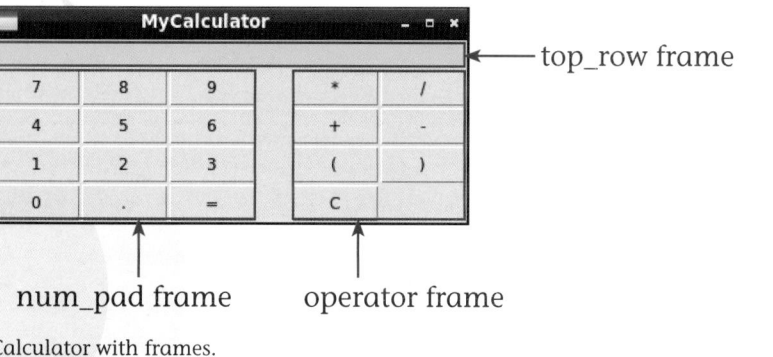

Calculator with frames.

> Some people specialise in laying out user interfaces for apps. If they are good at their jobs, their interfaces always appear to be the natural solution to the user.

If you look carefully at the code you should see how the frame widgets are arranged in the window and the buttons are then grouped in the frames.

for loops

In *Python Basics* we learned about **while loops**. Now it is time to meet for loops. A **for loop** is great when handling lists, dictionaries or tuples. For loops go through the indented code as many times as required, so in this case once for each button we need. That is, once for each value of btn_text. The variable btn_text is used to hold the values of the num_pad_list. So, on the first time round the loop, btn_text represents the string '7'. On the next time round btn_text will be '8'. Each time through the loop the column counter c is increased by 1 until it is greater than 2.

Experiment

Try running the code as supplied and then alter the code so that the column counter counts up until it is greater than 3 and see what happens. Keep altering the values of `c` and `r` until you have a good feel for how this loop builds the number pad.

The `num_pad_list` could all have been typed out on one line. See how much easier it is to read by adding line breaks. Line returns in lists, dictionaries and tuples are ignored by the computer.

Debugging

The code for each button should all make sense to you now. The problem here is: why doesn't this code work as expected? Working out why code does not work as expected is called **debugging**. There are two clues:

Clue 1: Nothing happens when we press the buttons.
Clue 2: The output when the app is first run is `7894561230.=`

? Quick Quiz 3.2

What do you notice about this output?
1 It is just random numbers and symbols?
2 The numbers and symbols are in the reverse order of the `num_pad_list`.
3 The numbers and symbols are in the same order as the `num_pad_list`.

The first clue tells us that the command option that links to our `click()` function does not work when we press the buttons. The second clue tells us that the function *was* called every time a button was created. tkinter is following a standard evaluation rule here: a function runs straight away if it is called with brackets after its name. However, we want to attach the function to the button ready to be called only if the button is pressed. For this to happen the tkinter button widget requires us to type the function's name without the brackets.

Try replacing `command=click(btn_text)` with `command=click` and then running the application. What do you think will happen? All is well until you press a button. We have solved the first problem – the `click()` function is no longer called as we create each button. When you do press a button though, the `click()` function is still not called. Other than this quite major problem, this is a much better way of designing our program than writing 19 button calls and 19 separate functions.

Building the calculator for real

The Investigation 2 file you have been working on may have a few bugs by now. If this is the case you can simply start with the fresh file `myCalculator3_start.py` from the Chapter 3 folder or check your code against this file and add the **commenting** backbone to the code from our experiments. Try running it to check that it behaves as you expect: the buttons still don't work! To finish the chapter we are going to ignore the fact that the buttons do not work and instead finish the layout so at least it looks like a calculator.

Your calculator now needs some buttons that perform operations such as adding, multiplying etc. These operator buttons need to be separated from the number pad. By choosing a large width for the display text box, we have made a space ready for this set of new buttons.

Add the code from Code Box 3.4 to `myCalculator_start.py` so that you have a complete set of buttons – that don't do anything.

> I think I get it. Although none of the buttons work yet, we only have to solve the problem in one place in our code and then all the buttons will work.

```
# create operator_frame
operator = Frame(window)
operator.grid(row=1, column=1, sticky=E)

operator_list = [
'*', '/',
'+', '-',
'(', ')',
'C' ]

# create operator buttons with a loop
r = 0
c = 0
for btn_text in operator_list:
    Button(operator, text=btn_text, width=5,
            command=click).grid(row=r,column=c)
    c = c+1
    if c > 1:
        c = 0
        r = r+1

##### Run mainloop
window.mainloop()
```

Save your code and run it to check it looks good! OK, so none of the buttons work but at least we do not have to sort that out in 19 separate places. Will we be able to sort out this problem? You will have to wait until the next chapter to find out!

> Crikey, a cliffhanger in a book on writing computer code!

Chapter summary

In this chapter you have:

- learned about for loops
- used lists and loops, saving a lot of repetitive coding
- learned a little more about the tkinter Button widget
- made a calculator application called MyCalculator that looks good but is not finished
- built a complex GUI quickly and easily.

This chapter has been about how to lay out a graphical user interface (GUI) with lots of buttons. In it, you added many buttons and organised them into groups using columns, rows and frames.

The ideas and puzzles this time are to help you get used to this process.

> My favourite kind of buttons are chocolate buttons.

Idea

Make a small calculator. Change the width of every button and then adjust the display width until your calculator looks good but is smaller.

Puzzle 1

Try to swap around the number pad with the function pad.

Puzzle 2

Add a button at the bottom of MyCalculator that is the full width of the calculator.
(**Hint**: this will require a new frame and then a new button. There is no need for a loop.)

Chapter 4
A fully working calculator

In this chapter you will:

- learn how to use default values in functions creatively

- learn about debugging

- learn about catching and handling errors

- delve deeper into binary numbers

- produce a fully working calculator.

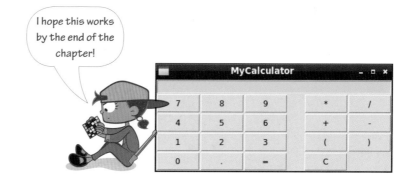

Arguments

In the last chapter we saw that the Button widget requires us to supply a function name without brackets. This is so that the function is called when the button is pressed and not when the button is built. Unfortunately, the neat use of a for loop has made it more difficult to send an argument to the `click()` function. We need to do this to tell it which button we are referring to. If we are not allowed to use brackets, we cannot directly supply an argument!

? Quick Quiz 4.1

What do arguments have to do with programming?
1 Arguments are another word for the keys in dictionaries.
2 Arguments are the values passed to a function.
3 Arguments are the values in a tuple.

To solve this problem we must send an argument indirectly! We can take advantage of how a function's arguments can be given **default** values. To remind you how this works try entering the code from Code Box 4.1 in interactive mode. (Don't forget that the code box shows both your input (after `>>>`) and the response from the program (in `blue`.) Then play with it until you can see how it works. The first two lines define a very simple function.

Code Box 4.1

```
>>> def my_function(x="default text"):
        print(x)
>>> my_function("two")
two
>>> my_function(3)
3
>>> my_function()
default text
```

This leads to quite an elegant solution. Open myCalculator4_start.py from the Chapter 4 folder and notice how there is a new function inserted into the loop called cmd(). You can also see this in Code Box 4.2. So how does it work? This is quite complicated but often when coding we do not need to understand how everything works. We can just use a solution that someone else has worked out. This is much like a mobile phone manufacturer fitting a processor chip to do a job without understanding how it does it. Nevertheless if you want an explanation see the Delving Deeper box.

Delving Deeper

In Code Box 4.2 you can see that the cmd() function sets the value held by btn_text as a default value of x. This allows the cmd() function to be called without supplying any arguments and that means it will still work without brackets supplied when it is used as the command for all the buttons made inside the loop. When cmd() is called by pressing a particular button on the calculator it in turn calls click() with its default btn_text value supplied. So now the click() function knows which button is being sent to it.

My brain hurts! However I am going to add this to my list of code snippets. It looks like it could be useful in the future!

Code Box 4.2

```
# create num_pad buttons with a loop
r = 0
c = 0
for btn_text in num_pad_list:
    def cmd(x=btn_text):
        click(x)
    Button(num_pad, text=btn_text, width=5, command=cmd).grid(row=r,column=c)
    c = c+1
    if c > 2:
        c = 0
        r = r+1
```

If you run this script you will find that the number buttons on your calculator now work as expected. Now see if you can alter the code in `operator_list` so that these buttons also put text into the calculator's display. An answer, in case you need it, is in Code Box 4.3.

Note how in Code Box 4.3 `btn_text` has been replaced by `b`. This is quicker to write but more difficult to understand. You will often see code like this but you should stick to using descriptive variable names except for counters such as `r` and `c`.

Code Box 4.3

```
# create operator buttons with a loop
r = 0
c = 0
for b in operator_list:
    def cmd(x=b):
        click(x)
    Button(operator, text=b, width=5, command=cmd).grid(row=r,column=c)
    c = c+1
    if c > 1:
        c = 0
        r = r+1
```

When you run the application now, all the buttons send a call to the `click()` function via `cmd()` and successfully pass along the correct button label. So finally we can put all of the code for how each button works in one place.

Perfecting the click() function

The calculator has three types of buttons:

- buttons that add content to the display

- the equals button that evaluates what is in the display

- the C button that clears the screen.

Most of the buttons just print their value in the calculator's display. Therefore after handling the behaviour of all the other buttons we can leave this code in the

It is good code design to separate out appearance from function in your applications. The calculator is constructed separately from the `click()` function. The `click()` function is where all the work occurs.

`else` clause at the bottom of the function. You can now add the code from Code Box 4.4 to your `myCalculator4_start.py` file. You should find that it mostly does as you would expect.

Code Box 4.4

```python
# key press function:
def click(key):
    # pressing equals key means calculate:
    if key == "=":
        result = str(eval(display.get()))
        display.insert(END, " = " + result)
    # pressing C key means clear screen:
    elif key == "C":
        display.delete(0, END)

    # add other key-pressed values to end of current entry:
    else:
        display.insert(END, key)
```

Analysis of Code Box 4.4

The code after the `else:` **statement** is the same as we had before. It inserts the value or symbol of the button at the end of `display`, which is our text entry box widget functioning as our display.

The code that handles the clear key (after the `elif` statement) deletes everything in `display` from the first character (the character at position 0) through to the end.

The interesting stuff happens when the equals button is pressed (after the `if` statement). Here we take advantage of the fact that the Python language is pretty good at maths itself.

The line that starts `result` does the maths and the next line of code adds an equals sign to the display and then the result of the calculation. This leaves us with one line of quite complicated code to explain – the one that does the maths.

```
result = str(eval(display.get()))
```

Basically, this line of code works out the answer of the contents of `display` and stores it in a variable which we name `result`.

Did you know that changing one data type into another like this is called casting?

MyCalculator				
7*3=21				
7	8	9	*	/
4	5	6	+	-
1	2	3	(	)
0	.	=	C	

Calculator with a calculation in the display.

The way this works is by applying a series of functions at the same time. For example, the result of the `eval()` function is a float or integer data type. The Entry widget only accepts strings so we use the `str()` function to change the float result into a string.

Nesting function calls within other function calls like this saves typing but can be difficult to read. Here is another way of representing the same code in more than one line so that it is a lot easier to understand:

```
result = display.get() # store the contents of entry in a variable
result = eval(result) # use the eval() function to do the calculation
result = str(result) # cast result to a string.
```

This takes a lot more typing though!

Testing and debugging

The calculator is nearly finished. The next stage is to test it thoroughly and note down the problems. Try the following calculations and put them in a debugging table like the one below.

Test calculations:

7*2,   7/2,   7+2,   7−2,   7*(7+2),   10/2,   10/6,   10/3,   7*(7+2))

Sum	Output	OK?
7*2	14	✓
7/2	3.5	✓

Table 4.1 The start of a debugging table.

Two problems should emerge from this process:

- Any unexpected input such as an extra bracket produces an error in the console and no response in the calculator.

- The results of some division calculations are unexpected (e.g. 10/3 produces 3.3333333333333335 where we would expect 3.3333333333333333).

Catching errors

We can solve the first problem with a common coding technique we met first in Chapter 2: we catch errors and handle them with helpful messages. In Python this is done by putting the function that might not work after a `try:` clause. We then handle the error, if there is one, after an `except:` clause.

You should now alter your `click()` method so it looks like the code in Code Box 4.5.

Code Box 4.5

```python
# key press function:
def click(key):
    # pressing equals key means calculate:
    if key == "=":
        try:
            result = str(eval(display.get()))
            display.insert(END, " = " + result)
        except:
            display.insert(END, " --> Error!")

    # pressing C key means clear screen:
    elif key == "C":
        display.delete(0, END)

    # add other key-pressed values to end of current entry:
    else:
        display.insert(END, key)
```

Now run this and see how it handles any entry that does not actually make sense such as 7*(7+2)), which has an extra bracket.

The second problem we have to solve is that when our calculator tries to work out 10/3 it unexpectedly rounds up at some point.

It is very important to try and think of all the unusual things that users could try in your applications and sort them out if your apps are not going to constantly go wrong.

I have a particular talent at thinking up strange things you could do with apps!

Wow Mr Campbell, I thought doing division in base 10 was hard!

Binary division does not even appear in 'A' Level maths at the moment, so the Delving Deeper section is just for our readers who are gifted mathematicians.

Delving Deeper

Computers store numbers on silicon chips. Each location on the chip can either have a negative charge or not. This means computers normally do maths in base two (usually called binary), where each memory location is equal to either 0 or 1. It is as if you only had one finger on each hand! No other numbers are allowed. Here are some decimal numbers with their binary equivalents:

Decimal (base 10)	Binary
1	1
2	10
3	11
4	100
5	101
6	110
7	111
8	1000

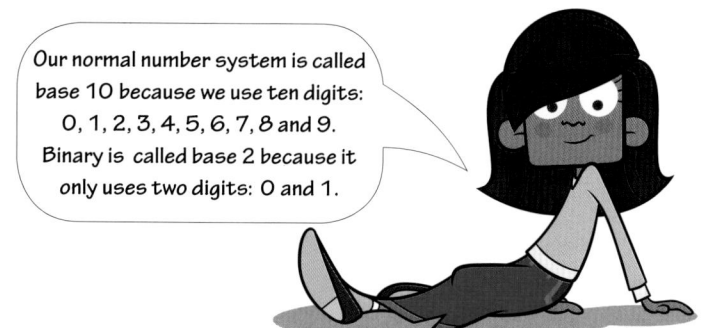

Our normal number system is called base 10 because we use ten digits: 0, 1, 2, 3, 4, 5, 6, 7, 8 and 9. Binary is called base 2 because it only uses two digits: 0 and 1.

The problem arises when computers try and represent 0.1 in base 10 as a **binary number**:

$\quad$ 0.1 (in base 10) = 0.00011001100110011001100 … (in binary)

This is the same as what happens when you divide two by three in base 10, which as a decimal equals 0.66666… . Unfortunately, it is not possible for computers to represent 0.1 accurately as a simple binary number either. This means it always has to be rounded at some point – which necessarily introduces some inaccuracy.

Computers normally do division this way:

1 Convert the two base 10 numbers to binary: 10/3 becomes 1010/11
2 Do the division in binary: 1010/11 = 11.01010101010 ... (At this point we require some rounding of the answer as otherwise it goes on for ever.)
3 Convert back to base 10: 3.33333333333333348136306995

Computers cannot easily do accurate division!

This turns out to be quite a complicated problem to solve – currently our calculator does all its division exactly this way.

There is an easy way to solve this problem. It is to give the answer to an acceptable number of decimal places, well before Python has done its rounding. We need to **slice** the result, like this:

```
result = display.get() # store the contents of entry in a variable
result = eval(result) # use the eval() function to do the calculation
result = str(result) # cast to a string.

# slice the result to show characters 0 to 10
# (ie 10 digits and a decimal point):
result = result[0:10]
```

The beauty of typing less

This can be written with far less code though – by nesting some of these function calls like this:

```
result = str(eval(display.get()))[0:10]
```

So now you can amend your calculator and test it by adjusting the file to incorporate the changes in Code Box 4.6. After making these changes and saving, you should have a fully functioning simple calculator.

Code Box 4.6

```
# myCalculator.py

from tkinter import *

# key press function:
def click(key):
    # pressing equals key means calculate:
    if key == "=":
        try:
            result = str(eval(display.get()))[0:10]
            display.insert(END, " = " + result)
        except:
            display.insert(END, " --> Error!")

    # pressing C key means clear screen:
    elif key == "C":
        display.delete(0, END)
    # add other key-pressed values to end of current entry:
    else:
        display.insert(END, key)
```

The calculator works! Ahem, I never doubted it.

Chapter summary

In this chapter you have:

- learned more about default values in functions
- learned some more about testing and debugging
- learned about catching and handling errors
- delved deeper into binary numbers and how computers do sums
- produced a fully working calculator
- learned how to slice strings.

After all that hard work, its time to play with the calculator before we start to show you how to customise it in the final two chapters.

Idea 1

Go back and try out your debugging table again and check that the calculator now handles all the test input as we would hope.

Idea 2

Try out your new calculator on some real problems. Then compare the answers with another calculator.

I love maths so much!

Idea 3

If you have never done any binary maths before, read the section on binary numbers in Appendix 2. This explains how to convert binary numbers to and from decimal numbers.

Idea 4

If you tried Idea 3 but decided not to read the Delving Deeper section earlier in this chapter…and if your brain does not ache yet – you could go back and read it now!

Chapter 5
Customising the calculator

In this chapter you will:

- lay out a customisable calculator

- create some fully functioning constant buttons

- start a module to hold the functions for our programmable buttons

- learn a little more about how to organise code in applications.

Adding more buttons

Calculators can sure have a lot of buttons!

In Chapter 4 you produced a simple calculator that does all the things that a normal calculator does. In this chapter you will add some more buttons that you can program to do exactly what you want.

Adding a set of buttons for constants

There is nothing new here. So let's just get typing!

Open `myCalculator5_start.py` from the Chapter 5 folder on the companion website. This contains a clean copy of the code we have produced so far with some comments indicating where to add the new bits of code. After having a quick look at the file to check you recognise everything, add the code from Code Box 5.1 where indicated.

Code Box 5.1

```
# create constants_frame
constants = Frame(window)
constants.grid(row=3, column=0, sticky=W)

constants_list = [
'pi',
'speed of light (m/s)',
'speed of sound (m/s)',
'ave dist to sun (km)' ]

# create constants buttons with a loop
r = 0
c = 0
```

```
for btn_text in constants_list:
    def cmd(x=btn_text):
        click(x)
    Button(constants, text=btn_text, width=22, command=cmd).grid(row=r, column=c)
    r = r+1
```

Notice that the new buttons we have added are for set values that do not change; for example, the speed of sound is a fixed scientific value. Therefore, these buttons are constants (you met constants in Chapter 2). If you run this script you will find that the constant buttons are now in the correct place and print their names in the calculator's display.

Adding a set of buttons for the functions

Let's look again at the image of our new and improved calculator:

The four buttons in the bottom right-hand corner are called function buttons because they apply a set function to a number you enter into the calculator. See if you can produce the code to make the function buttons. An answer is below in Code Box 5.2 but you should be able to do this yourself without looking. Use the code for the constants as your guide and think about what columns and rows you need.

The 'Roman' button on the calculator represents 'Roman numerals' – you know: i, ii, iii, etc.

Code Box 5.2

```
# create functions_frame
functions = Frame(window)
functions.grid(row=3, column=1, sticky=E)

functions_list = [
'factorial (!)',
'-> roman',
'-> binary',
'binary -> 10' ]

# create functions buttons with a loop
r = 0
c = 0
for b in functions_list:
    def cmd(x=b):
        click(x)
    Button(functions, text=b, width=13, command=cmd).grid(row=r, column=c)
    r = r+1
```

Now check that your calculator shows the names of all the new buttons.

Delving Deeper

The object here is to produce your very own calculator that does what you want. The functions in this book are unusual examples that might inspire you to attach functions that are not on everyone else's calculators. If however, you want to add some more traditional functions such as x^2 or $\sqrt{}$ they are easy to add using the $**$ operator that raises a number to a given power:

```
def square(n):
    return n**2

def square_root(n)
    return n**0.5
```

If you do not understand this ask your maths teacher.

Attaching the constants to the buttons

It is easy to attach the constants to the buttons. We will add the required code to the `click()` function by looking out for the new buttons with more `elif` statements. Continue amending `myCalculator5_start.py` by adding the new code from Code Box 5.3 and then test out the pi button. You will be adding your own constants in no time.

Code Box 5.3

```
    # now for the constant buttons:
    elif key == constants_list[0]:
        display.insert(END, "3.141592654")
```

Try to complete the others yourself. When the pi button works, try adding the code so that the other constant buttons work too. Here are their values:

- The speed of light: 300000000m/s.

- The speed of sound: 330m/s.

- The average distance to the sun: 149597887.5km.

If you are successful, the buttons should all work as expected. Check them out. If you have any difficulties that you cannot solve yourself, code that works is provided in Code Box 5.4.

Code Box 5.4

```
# now for the constant buttons:
elif key == constants_list[0]:
    display.insert(END, "3.141592654")
elif key == constants_list[1]:
    display.insert(END, "300000000")
elif key == constants_list[2]:
    display.insert(END, "330")
elif key == constants_list[3]:
    display.insert(END, "149597887.5")
```

My favourite constant is Avogadro's constant, which is:

602 200 000 000 000 000 000 000

Getting the function buttons organised

To keep our code as easy to read and as flexible as possible, we are going to store the functions in a separate file. You might remember from *Python Basics* that a file that contains functions is called a **module**. Can you remember what we do to make a module available to your apps? We import it. First, we need to add the line of code that will import this file, to the beginning of the program. We can then add lines of code to the click() function that will go and get the functions we require.

In the Chapter 5 folder in the source code from the companion website there is a module called calc_functions.py. It has a skeleton structure that provides functions that simply print out the name of the function buttons when they are pressed. You can examine it in Code Box 5.5.

Putting your functions in a separate module is a good idea because the module can be used to store lots of functions. You will never need to delete functions: they can be added or removed from your calculator by making a button as you wish. The functions will also be available to other applications if you need them in the future.

```
Code Box 5.5

# function module for calculator application in Python: Next Steps

# Factorial function:
def factorial(n):
    return "factorial (!)"

# Convert to roman numerals function:
def to_roman(n):
    return "-> roman"

# Convert base 10 numbers to binary function:
def to_binary(n):
    return "-> binary"
```

(continues on the next page)

```
# Convert base 2 numbers to base 10 function:
def from_binary(n):
    return "binary -> 10"
```

Your job now is to amend `myCalculator5_start.py` by replacing the first three lines by the contents of Code Box 5.6.

Code Box 5.6

```
# myCalculator.py

from tkinter import *
import calc_functions
```

Delving Deeper

There are two ways to import modules:

1 Use the structure: `import calc_functions`. When we use this, we must call the functions in our programs with a reference to that module: `calc_functions.factorial(n)`.

2 As we use the methods from the tkinter module so often, we choose to import it differently: `from tkinter import *`. This way of importing modules means that when we call a function from that module in our program we no longer need to precede it with a reference to that module file: `grid(row=r, column=c)`

Both systems are shown in this book because you will see examples of both in other Python code you meet. If you know what is going on you shouldn't get confused.

The code that calls the `factorial()` function when the factorial button on the calculator is pressed is supplied in Code Box 5.7. Currently, this takes the entry from the calculator display and returns the name of the button. Later on it will work out what the answer is. Add the code to call this function from Code Box 5.7 and try it out to see how this works.

Code Box 5.7

```
# now for the function buttons:
elif key == functions_list[0]:
    n = display.get() # collect display value
    display.delete(0, END) # clear display
    display.insert(END, calc_functions.factorial(n))
```

Before testing this, read it carefully and try to predict what you think will happen.

? Quick Quiz 5.1

What do we expect?
1 The answer will be calculated correctly.
2 There will be an error message.
3 The display will be cleared and the name of the button will appear.
4 The name of the button will be added to the end of the display.

Your job now is to sort out the other three buttons in the same way. Here are the function names in `calc_functions.py`:

- `to_roman(n)`
- `to_binary(n)`
- `from_binary(n)`

One way of doing this is shown in Code Box 5.8. It involves copying and pasting so could probably be improved. Try to work out what is required yourself before looking at this answer.

```
Code Box 5.8                                                    x

# now for the function buttons:
elif key == functions_list[0]:
    n = display.get() # collect display value
    display.delete(0, END) # clear display
    display.insert(END, calc_functions.factorial(n))

elif key == functions_list[1]:
    n = display.get() # collect display value
    display.delete(0, END) # clear display
    display.insert(END, calc_functions.to_roman(n))

elif key == functions_list[2]:
    n = display.get() # collect display value
    display.delete(0, END) # clear display
    display.insert(END, calc_functions.to_binary(n))

elif key == functions_list[3]:
    n = display.get() # collect display value
    display.delete(0, END) # clear display
    display.insert(END, calc_functions.from_binary(n))
```

I remember how to do this! `calc_functions.to_roman(n)` means 'run the `to_roman()` function in the `calc_functions` module and send it the value stored in n as its argument'.

From now on all we need to do is adjust the code in the `calc_functions.py` module.

Chapter summary

In this chapter you have:

- built the user interface for a customisable calculator
- created some fully functioning constant buttons
- imported a module that will hold the functions for our programmable buttons
- learned a little more about how to organise code in applications.

You now have a calculator with eight programmable buttons. And more importantly, you are already getting very good in the language that is used to program this calculator. The challenges below will encourage you to start this process.

Challenge 1

Choose one of the function buttons and rename it `square`. Then in the `calc_functions.py` file add the code to add this functionality. If you need to you can look back at page 65 in the Delving Deeper section to help you do this.

Challenge 2

Choose another one of the function buttons and rename it `sqrt`. Then in the `calc_functions.py` file add the code to add this functionality. Again you can look back at page 65 in the Delving Deeper section if you need to.

Challenge 3

Refactor the repetitive code in Code Box 5.7 so that the two repeating lines are only coded once.

Hint: You will need to have a separate `if elif elif else` structure inside a single `elif` statement.

Ideas

- Start to think about what you would like your calculator to be able to do in the future.
- Add some more code to the other two buttons that you think might be useful to you.
- Find out what the mathematical function factorial does.
- Use the calculator to work out how many minutes it takes light from the sun to get to Earth.
- See how far you can go when writing out Roman numerals without using our calculator.
- Practise converting binary numbers to decimals and back using the instructions in Appendix 2.
- Make a cute little calculator by changing all the button sizes again.
- Make a giant-screen-filling-monster of a calculator.

Sometimes you might see something like $1.8E+7$ in the calculator display. This means 1.8×10^7, which is another way of writing $18\,000\,000$.

What's next?

If you wish to stop here that is fine. You have a fully functioning calculator that you can customise by changing the constant buttons and the function buttons. If you are not going any further you might like to add some of the functions from the `calc_functions.py` file to your calculator. You can find the code in `calc_functions.py` on the companion website in the 'Final' folder that is within the 'Bonus Chapter' folder. There is also a copy of the final `calc_functions.py` file provided for you to study in Appendix 3.

The Bonus Chapter explains how computer scientists use algorithms to create functions like these. Although some of the material is quite hard, it is very interesting. Even if you do not understand it all, you will learn lots!

Bonus chapter
Algorithms

In this chapter you will:

- add code to the programmable buttons

- learn about algorithms

- complete the calculator project

- learn about factorials

- learn how to convert numbers to Roman numerals.

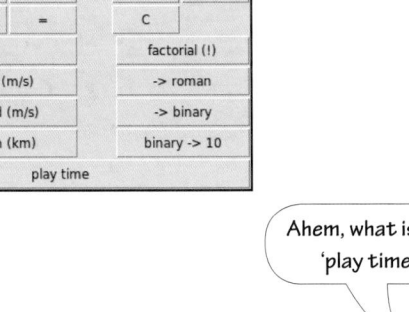

Ahem, what is this, 'play time'?!

An introductory note

In this chapter we are not going to alter the `myCalculator.py` file. However, when testing the calculator, this is still the file that needs to be opened and run. We will do the work of this chapter on the `calc_functions.py` script that you met for the first time in Chapter 5. You should begin with the files supplied in the sub-folder called 'Start' that can be found within the folder called 'Bonus Chapter' you have downloaded from the companion website. There is also a final version of the files `myCalculator.py` and `calc_functions.py` within the sub-folder called 'Final', but you should only refer to this if you get stuck. Please be aware this is an interesting but difficult chapter!

I cannot get through the day without at least one cappuccino.

Developing algorithms

An **algorithm** is a step-by-step recipe, or a set of rules, that solves a problem. For example, sorting a list of words into alphabetical order is an important thing for computers to do. There are many ways of solving this simple problem. A lot of research has gone into finding the most efficient algorithm because it is such an important task.

Here is an algorithm for making a cup of coffee:

1. Get a mug.
2. Add 1 teaspoon of instant coffee to the mug.
3. Add water to a kettle.
4. Boil the water.
5. Add the boiling water to the mug to within 2 cm of the top.
6. Get the milk from the fridge.
7. Add 1 cm depth of milk to the mug.
8. Put the milk back in the fridge.

These are the kind of precise instructions a computer or robot would require to make a cup of coffee. When creating computer applications we often use functions that have algorithms in them. There are a number of ways of doing this. Some coders write flow diagrams. Some just write it out as it comes to them and figure it out as they go along. Others try to write out the algorithm in simple terms first and then write the code. The 'just-write-it' method is not the best choice and often results in far more work in the end than the other two. In this chapter we write two algorithms and use a different approach to write each one.

The factorial function

Factorials may be new to you. In maths lessons we might write $5!$ and we would say 'five factorial'.

$5! = 5 \times 4 \times 3 \times 2 \times 1$

$\quad = 120$

You may be thinking that this will need a loop. Notice how you are now thinking like a coder. The method we will use this time is to have a first go at writing the algorithm and then turn it into code. Here is the algorithm:

1 Assign the target number to a variable: n.
2 Create a variable to store the answer: ans.
3 Make ans equal to n.
4 Reduce n by 1.
5 Make ans equal to itself times by n.
6 Continue doing this until n equals 1.

We should now be confident that we will be able to write some code to do this.

Open `calc_functions.py` from the 'Start' folder in the 'Bonus Chapter' folder and add the code from Code Box 6.1. Note this will produce an error when you run it. The Quick Quiz should help you work out why.

Code Box 6.1

```python
# Factorial function:
def factorial(n):
    ans=n # set initial value of answer before loop
    while n>1:
        ans=ans*(n-1)
        n=n-1
    return ans
```

? Quick Quiz 6.1

Why is our function not working?
1 The code works but produces the wrong answer.
2 The while loop never ends.
3 There is an error in the algorithm.
4 The calculator script is passing a string to the function rather than an integer.

The clue is in the last line of the error message. To solve this we need to add a line that casts the string into an integer. Fix this with the code in Code Box 6.2.

Code Box 6.2

```
# Factorial function:
def factorial(n):
    n=int(n) # cast the string argument to an integer
    ans=n # set initial value of answer before loop
    while n>1:
        ans=ans*(n-1)
        n=n-1
    return ans
```

Testing and debugging time

If you run the calculator now you should find that the factorial function works quite well. Did you know that 0! = 1. Our calculator doesn't!

Try to complete a debugging table, like you did in Chapter 4, to see if you can spot any other problems:

Test input:

5, 0, 7–2, 3.2, 50, 5+2 = 7

Entry	Expected result	Actual result
5	120	120
0	1	0

Table 6.1 The start of a debugging table.

This should throw up several issues:

- zero factorial is a special case
- if the number gets too large the answer does not fit on the screen and can cause the calculator to stop working
- you cannot have a factorial of a negative number
- you cannot have a factorial of a decimal number.

The bug fixes can be added by copying the code from Code Box 6.3 in place of the faulty code.

Code Box 6.3

```
# Factorial function:
def factorial(n):
    try:
        n = int(n)
    except:
        return "--> Error!"

    # '0' is special:
    if n == 0:
        return 1

    # back out if too large:
    if n > 40:
        return "--> Answer will not fit on screen!"
```

The number 40 was chosen by experimentation to see which number pushed the answer beyond the display. It was 41.

(continues on the next page)

```
#catch negative numbers:
if n < 0:
    return "--> Error!"

# apply factorial algorithm
ans=n # set initial value of answer before loop
while n > 1:
    ans = ans*(n-1)
    n = n-1
return ans
```

Analysis of Code Box 6.3

If the input from the display is not an **integer** we need to catch the error with `try`: `except`:

Next we solve the `0!` special case with an `if` clause.

We can solve the problem of large numbers in a similar way. This is important because large numbers ask the computer to work very hard and may cause the calculator to stop working.

Finally we have to deal with the negative numbers because they cannot produce a factorial. All we have to do is test for numbers less than zero.

The Roman numeral function

To convert an integer into a Roman numeral requires another algorithm. This time we will try and work out the code by using a flow diagram.

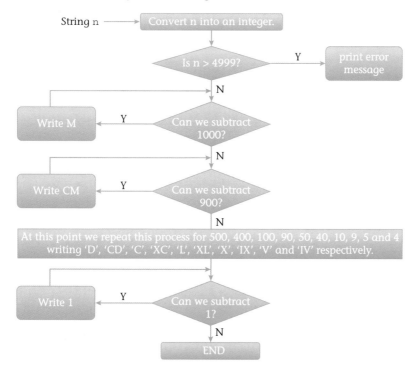

> Bigger numbers can be made by putting a bar over a letter. The bar indicates a 1000 times the normal value, so $\bar{V}$ is 5000 and $\bar{M}$ is a million.

Flow diagram for converting to Roman numerals.

Our flow diagram suggests we need a tuple to store the set of numbers: 1000, 900, 500, etc. so we can loop through them; we also need a dictionary to store which letter(s) they correspond to so we can look them up. This can be achieved in several ways without the need for many lines of code. Copy out the code from Code Box 6.4 into the correct place in `calc_functions.py` you have been working on. Think carefully about how it works as you type.

Challenge

It is too early in your programming knowledge to expect you to be able to do this without giving you the code in Code Box 6.4. But, if you are keen to try, then **do not look** at Code Box 6.4 as this is the answer! Instead, create the tuple and dictionary, use a for loop to go through the tuple and see if you can solve this tricky puzzle.

Code Box 6.4

```python
# Convert number to roman numerals:
def to_roman(n):
    try:
        n = int(n)
    except:
        return "--> Error!"

    # opt out of numbers greater than 4999:
    if n > 4999:
        return "--> out of range"

    # create the tuple and dictionary:
    numberBreaks = (1000,900,500,400,100,90,50,40,10,9,5,4,1)
    letters = {1000 : "M", 900 : "CM", 500 : "D", 400 : "CD", 100 : "C",
               90 : "XC", 50 : "L", 40 : "XL", 10 : "X", 9 : "IX", 5 : "V",
               4 : "IV", 1 : "I" }
```

```
# start the algorithm:
result = ""
for value in numberBreaks:
    while n >= value:
        result = result+letters[value]
        n = n-value
return result
```

At first I couldn't work this one out. It isn't too difficult to see how it works when you look through the solution though.

Analysis of Code Box 6.4

Although this is a tricky algorithm to convert into code, it introduces nothing that is new to you. To work out how this code works all you need to do is compare it carefully with the flow diagram on page 81.

The convert to binary function

Python already has functions that can be used to convert from one base to another, so this function is very simple to program. Although we will wrap it in `try:` and `catch:` you only need to focus on two lines of code:

```
n = int(n)
return bin(n)[2:]
```

The first line converts the string that is sent from the display to an integer.

What is the coder's word for converting one data type into another?
1 casting
2 throwing
3 catching

The second line uses Python's `bin()` function. This function returns a binary number as a string but precedes it with `0b`:

```
>>> bin(10)
'0b1010'
```

To display what we want, we must strip off the first two characters. Because the returned value from the `bin()` function is a string, we can simply **slice** it by adding `[2:]` after the function call. This says: only return the characters from index 2 and beyond. Just what we want!

Now copy the code from Code Box 6.5 into `calc_functions.py` to get this button working.

Code Box 6.5

```python
# Convert base 10 numbers to binary function:
def to_binary(n):
    try:
        n = int(n)
        return bin(n)[2:]
    except:
        return "--> Error!"
```

The final function

Again, Python already has a built-in function to cast to an integer, `int()`. Normally we do not give it any other argument other than a number string. If we are giving it a binary string we need to supply an optional argument which is the base. The default, if we do not supply it, is base 10 but we need to tell the `int()` function what we are doing if we supply a binary number:

```
>>> int("100", 2)
4
```

Now copy the code from Code Box 6.6 into `calc_functions.py` to finish your fully working programmable calculator.

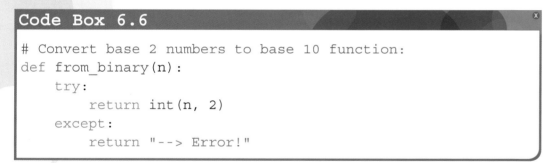

```
Code Box 6.6

# Convert base 2 numbers to base 10 function:
def from_binary(n):
    try:
        return int(n, 2)
    except:
        return "--> Error!"
```

There are many other functions that you can attach to your buttons. Instead of recoding them you could actually add more buttons if you prefer. A good place to start is to look at other calculators and see if there is anything that they do that you want your calculator to be able to do too.

Have fun!

Chapter summary

In this chapter you have:

- learned how to calculate factorials
- learned about algorithms
- added code to the programmable buttons
- found how to convert numbers to roman numerals
- learned more about casting
- completed the calculator project.

There are many options available to you now. The easiest changes to make are to the constant buttons. Below are a few other ideas.

Ideas

- Change the size of the calculator again by making the buttons smaller and tweaking the widths of the display.
- Change the colour of the display.
- Change the function buttons to some of your favourites.

Once you understand the basics of a programming language, it is an important skill to be able to look through other people's code and work out how it works. When you do this, do not worry if you do not understand everything. Just be ready to learn.

Just as with *Python Basics*, a bonus app is provided, which is called `myCalculatorPlus.py`. It can be found in the 'Bonus' folder in the 'Bonus Chapter' folder in the source code file (if you have not already peeked!). This adds a further button at the bottom of the calculator that runs a neat little game. This game is all about converting binary numbers to base 10.

When you press the 'play time' button you will find a binary number presented in the calculator display. The object of the game is to clear ten binary numbers as fast as you can. To clear the random binary number displayed press the calculator number key that corresponds to it. If you get it correct, a new number will appear. When you have completed ten numbers the game tells you how long you took.

This, of course, gives an opportunity to provide further ideas!

Further ideas

- Try to make the timer more accurate.
  Hint: Look out for the comment telling you where a string has been truncated to five characters.
- Make the game easier for younger children by turning it into a kind of 'whack-a-mole game' by displaying the actual button numbers that have to be hit, instead of the binary version.
- Change the game so that it shows a Roman numeral in the display and you have to hit the correct number button.

A harder idea

Make a copy of `myCalculatorPlus.py` and change the game so
that it does the following:
- Asks the player: 'Choose a times table to practise.'
- If the user has chosen the 5 times table then the calculator
  should randomly display a number from the set: 0, 5, 10, 15, 20,
  25, 30, 35, 40 and 45. To clear them and go onto the next one
  the user would type 0, 1, 2, 3, 4, 5, 6, 7, 8 or 9, respectively.

> Wow, this will really
> help me get fast at
> my times tables!

Puzzle

OK, so you think you can code now? Here is a serious challenge for you! If you look at the code for converting
numbers to Roman numerals you will see there is an unnecessary repeat of information. The values in the tuple
are also in the dictionary. Surely we do not need both? Well, you don't, but you will have to replace both with a
very useful construct: a tuple of tuples:

```
romans = (
        (1000, "M"), (900, "CM"), (500, "D"), (400, "CD"), (100, "C"), (90, "XC"),
        (50, "L"), (40, "XL"), (10, "X"), (9, "IX"), (5, "V"), (4, "IV"), (1, "I")
        )
```

Study this interactive session:

```
Python Shell                                          _ □ ✗

File   Edit   Debug   Options   Windows                          Help

Python 3.1.3 (r313:86834, Nov 28 2010, 10:01:07)
[GCC 4.4.5] on linux2
Type "copyright", "credits" or "license()" for more information.
==== No Subprocess ====
>>> romans = ((1000, "M"), (900, "CM"), (500, "D"), (400, "CD"), (100, "C"),
(90, "XC"), (50, "L"), (40, "XL"), (10, "X"), (9, "IX"), (5, "V"), (4, "IV"),
(1, "I"))
>>>
>>> romans
((1000, 'M'), (900, 'CM'), (500, 'D'), (400, 'CD'), (100, 'C'), (90, 'XC'),
(50, 'L'), (40, 'XL'), (10, 'X'), (9, 'IX'), (5, 'V'), (4, 'IV'), (1, 'I')
)
>>>
>>> romans[0]
(1000, 'M')
>>>
>>> romans[0][0]
1000
>>>
>>> romans[0][1]
'M'
>>>
>>> len(romans)
13
>>>

                                                      Ln: 14 Col: 4
```

Now rewrite the Roman numerals code in `calculator_functions.py` so that it uses the tuple of tuples rather than a tuple and a dictionary.

Good luck. There is an answer provided on the companion website, if you get stuck.

Taking things further

When you have finished this book we hope you will want to continue to learn to code. Here are some other places and resources you might like to look.

More Python

Other books in the series, found at the companion website (www.codingclub.co.uk).

The official Python documentation: http://docs.python.org/py3k/

The Python chapter in the Raspberry Filling guide:
http://downloads.raspberrypi.org/Raspberry_Pi_Education_Manual.pdf.

PyGame website: this site provides a set of modules that need to be downloaded that help with making games. It has a community of Python coding enthusiasts and enables you to post your games for others to play. Find it at www.pygame.org/

Other programming languages

A great next programming language might be Java. Java is very similar to the languages in the C family and would provide you with your first taste of a language that uses curly brackets. There are some great resources available. Perhaps the best place to start might be with Greenfoot. Java makes extensive use of classes and objects though, so you might prefer to do this after reading *Python: Building Big Apps*. This more advanced book introduces these concepts in Python which you are already familiar with.

Java Programming: www.greenfoot.org/

Appendix 1

Some key bits of information

The companion website

Website: www.codingclub.co.uk

The companion website has the answers to the puzzles and challenges in the book, and the complete source code including start files and bonus code. You will also find information about other books in the series, character profiles and much, much more.

Adding a series of buttons with a for loop

```
for btn_text in button_list:
    def cmd(x=btn_text):
        # The function attached to the button with its label passed as an argument:
        click(x)
    Button(num_pad, text=btn_text, width=5, command=cmd)
```

Catching errors

```
def my_function(args):
    try:
        # your code goes here
    except:
        return "--> Error!"
```

tkinter widgets

label ——————→
entry ——————→
button ——————→

label ——————→
text box ——————→

Here is some outline code for some widgets inside a window object called `window` created
with this line of code:

```
window = Tk()
```

```
my_frame = Frame(window)
my_label = Label(my_frame, text="My text goes here")
my_text_entry_box = Entry(my_frame, width=20, bg="light green")
my_button = Button(my_frame, text="SUBMIT", width=5,
                   command=[the function name to be called goes here])
my_text_box = Text(my_frame, width=75, height=6, wrap=WORD, background="light green")
```

Container data type summary

The table below provides a list of useful functions that you can use on strings, tuples, lists
and dictionaries. The table below assumes these containers have been created:

```
>>> s = "bar" # a string
>>> t = ("b", "a", "r") # a tuple
>>> l = ["b", "a", "r"] # a list
>>> d = {1:"b", 2:"a", 3:"r"} # a dictionary
```

Function	Strings	Tuples	Lists	Dictionaries
print all	`>>> print(s)` `bar`	`>>> print(t)` `('b', 'a', 'r')`	`>>> print(l)` `['b', 'a', 'r']`	`>>> print(d)` `{1: 'b', 2: 'a', 3: 'r'}`
print element	`>>> print(s[2])` `r`	`>>> print(t[2])` `r`	`>>> print(l[2])` `r`	`>>> print(d[2])` `a`

combine	`>>> a=s+"f"`
	 `>>> a`
	 `'barf'`
		`>>> a=t+("f",)`
		 `>>> a`
		 `('b', 'a', 'r', 'f')`
			`>>> a=l+["f"]`
			 `>>> a`
			 `['b', 'a', 'r', 'f']`	

add an element	Strings cannot be altered.	Tuples cannot be altered.	`>>> l.append("f")`
			 `>>> l`
			 `['b', 'a', 'r', 'f']`
				`>>> d[4]="f"`
				 `>>> d[4]`
				 `'f'`

sort	Strings cannot be altered.	Tuples cannot be altered.	`>>> l.sort()`
			 `>>> l`
			 `['a', 'b', 'r']`
				`>>> sorted(d)`
				 `['1', '2', '3']`
				 `>>> sorted(d.values())`
				 `['a', 'b', 'r']`

delete an element	Strings cannot be altered.	Tuples cannot be altered.	`>>> del l[1]`
			 `>>> l`
			 `['b', 'r']`
				`>>> del d[1]`
				 `>>> i`
				 `{2:'a', 3:'r'}`

replace element	Strings cannot be altered.	Tuples cannot be altered.	`>>> l[0]="c"`
			 `>>> l`
			 `['c', 'a', 'r']`
				`>>> d[1]="c"`
				 `>>> print(d)`
				 `{1: 'c', 2: 'a', 3: 'r'}`

find	`>>> i.find("b")` `0`	`>>> t.index("b")` `0`	`>>> l.index("b")` `0`	
get length	`>>> len(s)` `3`	`>>> len(t)` `3`	`>>> len(l)` `3`	`>>> len(d)` `3`

Table A1 Some useful functions.

Appendix 2

Binary numbers

To understand binary numbers it is best to remind ourselves how base 10 numbers work. Each column, starting from the right, stores values that are 10 times as large as the previous column.

e.g. The number 347 has 7 units, 4 tens, 3 hundreds and no thousands:

thousands	hundreds	tens	units
	3	4	7

So we get 347 by adding:

$$(3 \times 100) \quad + \quad (4 \times 10) \quad + \quad (7 \times 1)$$

In binary, or base 2 as it is sometimes called, the system is the same except each column is worth two times the preceding column:

e.g. 1101 (or 13 in base 10) has 1 unit, zero twos, 1 four, and 1 eight:

eights	fours	twos	units
1	1	0	1

So we can see 1101 in binary is 13 in base 10 by adding:

$$(1 \times 8) \quad + \quad (1 \times 4) \quad + \quad (0 \times 2) \quad + \quad (1 \times 1)$$

Thus if you want to work out what the value of a binary number is in base 10 you can write on your fingers and work it out like this:

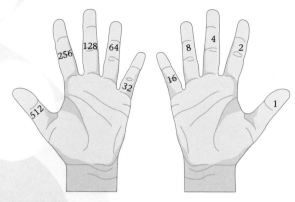

So 1101 can be represented like this:

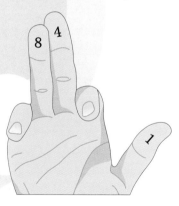

Appendix 3

Calculator functions source code

```python
# calc_functions.py
# function module for calculator application in Python: Next Steps

# Calculate the factorial of a number:
def factorial(n):
    try:
        n = int(n)
    except:
        return "--> Error!"

    # '0' is special:
    if n == 0:
        return 1

    # back out if too large:
    if n > 40:
        return "--> Answer will not fit on screen!"

    # catch negative numbers:
    if n < 0:
        return "--> Error!"

    # apply factorial algorithm:
```

```
        ans=n # set initial value of answer before loop
        while n > 1:
            ans = ans*(n-1)
            n = n-1
        return ans

# Convert number to roman numerals:
def to_roman(n):
    try:
        n = int(n)
    except:
        return "--> Error!"

    # opt out of numbers greater than 4999:
    if n > 4999:
        ans = "--> out of range"
        return ans

    # start algorithm:
    numberBreaks = (1000,900,500,400,100,90,50,40,10,9,5,4,1)
    letters = {1000 : "M", 900 : "CM", 500 : "D", 400 : "CD", 100 :
                "C", 90 : "XC", 50 : "L", 40 : "XL",
                10 : "X", 9 : "IX", 5 : "V", 4 : "IV",
                1 : "I" }
    result = ""
    for value in numberBreaks:
        while n >= value:
            result = result+letters[value]
            n = n-value
    return result
```

(continues on the next page)

```python
# Convert base 10 numbers to binary function:
def to_binary(n):
    try:
        n = int(n)
        return bin(n)[2:]
    except:
        return "--> Error!"

# Convert base 2 numbers to base 10 function:
def from_binary(n):
    try:
        return int(n, 2)
    except:
        return "--> Error!"
```

Glossary and index

algorithm step-by-step instructions to perform a task that a computer can understand 75

argument a piece of information that is required by a function so that it can perform its task; usually a string or number, `my_function(arguments go here)` 29

binary number a number represented in base 2 56

bug a piece of code that is causing a program to fail to run properly or at all 28

casting the process of converting one data type into another; e.g. sometimes a number is stored as text but may need to be converted into an integer – this can be done like this: `int("3")` 53

commenting some text in a computer program that is for the human reader and is ignored by the computer when running the program – in Python all comments begin with a hash symbol # 44

constant a number that does not change; it is good practice to name constants in capitals e.g. `SPEED_OF_LIGHT` 31

container container data types store groups of other data types, which may include more containers; the containers used in this book are tuples, lists and dictionaries 7

data types different types of information stored by the computer, for example floats, integers, strings, tuples, lists and dictionaries 7

integers	number data types that cannot have decimal values and must be whole numbers	7
interactive mode	this is when we use IDLE to try out snippets of code without saving them	14
key	the equivalent of an index in a string, tuple or list but for a dictionary; it is defined by the programmer and can, for example, be a string, integer, float or even a tuple in a `key:value` pair	15
list	an ordered container data type which can hold values of any type and can have elements added or removed; like a tuple each element is indexed from 0	14
loop	a piece of code that keeps repeating until a certain condition is met	39
method	the name given to a function in a class	13
module	a saved Python file whose functions can be used by another program	9
operator	a symbol that performs a simple function on some code such as multiplying two numbers or comparing them to see if they are equal; see also **equals operator**	26
ordered containers	ordered containers are container data types where the values stored are indexed together with their position in the container, e.g. tuples and lists; a dictionary is an example of an unordered container	17
output	data that is sent from a program to a screen or printer etc	8
refactoring	the process of changing the structure of code so it is less repetitive, more readable, easier to maintain, etc	39

return	(1) the value a function will produce after it has been run – it is also a Python keyword; (2) the 'end of line' key on a keyboard, sometimes called the enter key	12
slice	the process of extracting sections of a string or container variable – sometimes called array slicing	57
statement	used to mean a snippet of code; strictly speaking it is a piece of code that represents a command or action, e.g. a print statement	52
strings	text data that can be stored in a variable	7
tkinter	a package of classes that are often imported into Python programs that give methods that are useful for producing windows, drawing images and producing animations	22
tuple	an ordered container data type whose values are indexed from 0; its contents cannot be changed	8
value	anything that can be stored in a variable such as the elements in a container data type	8
variable	a name that refers to a place in a computer's memory where data is stored; more loosely, it can also be used to refer to that data	12
while loops	a kind of loop that repeats code while a comparing statement returns `True`	42
widget	an element of a GUI such as a button or text entry box	24

Some useful words

comparative operator   sometimes called logic operators, they allow us to compare data in a program; they include == and > (you can find others in Table 3 in the Appendix in Python Basics)

local variable   a variable that is defined inside a function and is only usable inside that function

mathematical operator   an operator that performs some mathematical function on some numbers, e.g. multiplication or addition

parameter   another word for argument when being used in a function

global variable   a variable that is usable anywhere in a program

hacking   taking some previously written code and rewriting bits to make it do something different

IDE   stands for Integrated Development Environment; IDLE is an example of one – they are special text editors with useful tools built in for programmers

IDLE   stands for Integrated DeveLopment Environment; this is the IDE that comes with a normal Python 3 install

infinite loop   a piece of code that keeps running forever; this is usually a bad thing

execute   another word for run – to execute some code is to run it

script mode   this is when we use IDLE to help us write code that we will save in a file

syntax error   an error produced when a computer fails to run a program because it cannot recognise the format of the code supplied, e.g. a syntax error would be produced if a closing bracket was missing

The Quick Quiz answers

Quick Quiz 1.1

1 Tuple.
2 List.
3 Tuple.

Quick Quiz 1.2

1 Dictionary.
2 Tuple.
3 Dictionary.
4 List.

Quick Quiz 3.1

Because we have called the `click()` function with brackets it will be called when the calculator buttons are created rather than when they are pressed. The problem now is: How do we supply an argument without brackets?

Quick Quiz 3.2

Answer = 3

Quick Quiz 4.1

Answer = 2

Quick Quiz 5.1

Answer = 3

Quick Quiz 6.1

Answer = 4

Quick Quiz 6.2

Answer = 1

Acknowledgements

It takes a great deal of effort to ensure that there are as few errors as possible appear in these books. The typesetters, for example, have a difficult job ensuring that every space is counted and colour change is made in the code boxes. My thanks go to Alex Bradbury, Marjory Bisset, Anna Littlewood, Carl Saxton and Heather Mahy who have all helped immensely with this process. Their care and attention to detail is greatly appreciated.

Producing three books in one year while holding down a full-time job can become all consuming and this asks a lot from my family. My wife Rita and son Daniel's patience with my obsession is never taken for granted. Unfortunately my work colleagues also have to put up with me occasionally mentioning this project. They never cease to act interested and are a great source of encouragement to me, so my thanks go to all the staff at Ewell Castle (except Mr. Blencowe who has ribbed me mercilessly).

The author and publisher acknowledge the following sources of copyright material and are grateful for the permissions granted.

p. 7 Image Zoo/Alamy; p. 20 Mau Hong/Shutterstock

The publisher has used its best endeavours to ensure that the URLs for external websites referred to in this book are correct and active at the time of going to press. However, the publisher has no responsibility for the websites and can make no guarantee that a site will remain live or that the content is or will remain appropriate.